P9-CND-357

CHRISTMAS
UNWRAPPED

CHRISTMAS
UNWRAPPED

A KID'S WINTER WONDERLAND OF HOLIDAY TRIVIA

Amy Shields

WITH CRAFTS BY
Kathy Ross

Sky Pony Press
NEW YORK

Sky Pony Press books may be purchased in bulk at special discounts for sales promotion, corporate gifts, fund-raising, or educational purposes. Special editions can also be created to specifications. For details, contact the Special Sales Department, Sky Pony Press, 307 West 36th Street, 11th Floor, New York, NY 10018 or info@skyhorsepublishing.com.

Sky Pony Press® is a registered trademark of Skyhorse Publishing, Inc.®, a Delaware corporation.

Visit our website at www.skyhorsepublishing.com.

Manufactured in China, June 2011
This product conforms to CPSIA 2008

1 3 5 7 9 10 8 6 4 2

Library of Congress Cataloging-in-Publication Data is available on file.
ISBN: 978-1-61608-469-1

Contents

Here Comes Santa!

Who is the big guy in the red suit? Of course you know! Over the years his name has changed, and so has the way he looks. He was a real person named Nicholas who was born in Turkey and became a bishop, and then a saint. He is the patron saint of children. He must have been a very special person to be remembered through history for 1,700 years. His birthday is celebrated each year on December 6.

On St. Nicholas Day, in many countries around the world, someone dressed as St. Nicholas visits children, bringing them small gifts. In Spain and the Netherlands, St. Nicholas checks in with boys and girls to see who's been naughty or nice. Their name for him is Sinterklass. When the Dutch came to settle in New York, Sinterklass became Santa Claus.

The legend of St. Nicholas has traveled a long way around the world and down through time to become our Santa Claus. Here's what St. Nicholas looked like back then (see left) and here is Santa Claus now!

Why does our Santa look like he does?

It's because of a poem and a picture. We didn't used to have an American version of Santa. "A Visit from St. Nicholas," written in 1823, changed all that. The poem captured people's imaginations. The poet Clement Clarke Moore names St. Nicholas in the poem, but his description is of a jolly old man that we all now think of as Santa:

> His eyes—how they twinkled! his dimples how merry!
> His cheeks were like roses, his nose like a cherry!
> His droll little mouth was drawn up like a bow
> And the beard of his chin was as white as the snow.

And the things this bearded old man in red did! Jumping down chimneys! Riding a sleigh pulled by flying reindeer! Bringing us presents! This was a Santa we could all love. Luckily, the poem inspired Thomas Nast. Mr. Nast was a cartoonist. In 1881, he drew a picture of Santa Claus (see right) that looks old-fashioned to us now, but is the great-great-grandpa of our Santa today.

How can Santa be everywhere at once?

During the holiday season, you probably see different Santas around your town or city. They might not look exactly like Santa or like each other. Some are fat and some are thin; some are tall and some are short—but they are always dressed in a red suit and white-trimmed hat, and they usually have a nice white beard. Santa can't be everywhere at once, so he has lots of look-alikes at Christmastime to remind us that he is watching to see who is naughty and who is nice.

If Santa's sleigh carried one toy for each boy and girl on the planet, it would weigh 400,000 tons and need almost 1 billion reindeer to pull it. To deliver all the presents in one night, Santa would have to visit 1,500 homes a second. Maybe some of those extra Santas you see around are the real deal?

Find the Different Santa Game

Look closely at these Santas. Two of them are missing something the rest have. Can you find them? One Santa is pretending to be a pirate.

Christmas Jokes

1. What is Tarzan's favorite Christmas carol?
2. What does Santa do in the summer?
3. What do snowmen eat for breakfast?
4. Why did the Christmas cookie go to the doctor?
5. Why do reindeer have fur coats?
6. How did the chickens dance at the Christmas party?
7. What do you give a reindeer with an upset tummy?

Santa Claus Tissue Box

Here is what you need:
- Square-shaped tissue box with tissue still in it • Cotton balls
- Red, white, black, and pink craft foam or construction paper
- Scissors • White tacky glue

Here is what you do:
1. Turn the tissue box on its side and pull the first tissue partway out to create the beard for the Santa.
2. Cut a triangle-shaped hat from the red craft foam. Glue the hat to the edge of the box above the beard.
3. Cut two cheeks from the pink craft foam, eyes from the white and black craft foam, and a nose from the red craft foam. Glue the facial features on the space between the hat and the beard.
4. Fluff out the cotton balls to make hair on each side of the face and fur trim along the bottom and tip of the hat.

Why does Santa come down the chimney?

Because at first he was just a little elf. It's true. In the poem "A Visit from St. Nicholas," Santa Claus is a *little* elf with a *little* mouth and a *little* belly. He rides a *miniature* sleigh pulled by *tiny* reindeer. He and his reindeer land on the roof, and he easily slips down the chimney. As small as he was, it would have been hard for him to reach a doorknob.

Thomas Nast drew him as he was described in the poem, and also made drawings of things that weren't in the poem. He imagined the North Pole workshop,

Santa's desk, and his Naughty/Nice book.

As the years went by, other artists drew Santa as they imagined him, and almost all of them pictured him as big and tall, so Santa grew up. Now that he can reach the doorknob, what do you think? Does he come through the door? Or do you think he actually tries to fit down the chimney?

A Merry Christmas

Who are Santa's helpers?

First of all, Santa's sleigh is pulled by eight tiny reindeer. They are a big help. We first learned about them in the poem "A Visit from St. Nicholas." The story of Rudolph, the ninth and smallest reindeer with the big red nose, came later. A big department store named Montgomery Ward gave away coloring books at Christmastime. In 1939, they decided to make their own book and had an employee named Robert May write a story about a reindeer. In the first year, they gave out 2.4 million copies of the book. The song about Rudolph came ten years later.

Mrs. Claus first appeared in 1849 in a short story. People don't read the story so much anymore, but Mrs. Claus is often pictured dressed like Santa, and looking a bit like him, too. The fact that they both

live at the North Pole with elves who help in the workshop is all pure Disney. In 1932, Walt Disney made a short film called *Santa's Workshop*, which showed the elves and the busy workshop. The film is still shown on television in Sweden every Christmas Eve. It has become part of their Christmas tradition.

Pipe Cleaner Reindeer Pin

Here is what you need:
- 12-inch (30-cm) brown pipe cleaner
- Red pom-pom • Two wiggle eyes
- Brown felt scrap • Small jingle bell
- Thin red craft ribbon • Pin back
- Scissors • White tacky glue

Here is what you do:
1. Cut a 6-inch (15-cm) piece of brown pipe cleaner. Fold the pipe cleaner at the center to form a V shape.
2. Cut a second piece of pipe cleaner 3 inches (7.5 cm) long. Place the piece across the V shape

about one third of the way up. Wrap the pipe cleaner around both stems of the V. Fold the leftover ends of the second pipe cleaner back to form the ears for the reindeer.

3. Cut the remaining piece of pipe cleaner in half. Wrap a piece around the top part of each side of the V to form the antlers for the reindeer.

4. Cut a triangle of brown felt to cover the back part of the head portion of the reindeer. Glue the felt in place behind the head.

5. Glue the red pom-pom on the point of the V for the nose. Glue the two wiggle eyes above the nose.

6. String a 6-inch (15-cm) piece of the red ribbon through the jingle bell. Tie the jingle bell to the top of one antler. Tie the ribbon in a bow and trim any excess ribbon from the ends.

7. Glue a pin back to the back of the reindeer.

All the Trimmings

People who celebrate Christmas often spend lots of time getting ready for the big day. A wreath goes on the front door, cards are written, and a tree is brought home and put up to be decorated. Boxes come out of the closet or down from the attic so that Christmas stockings and ornaments can be unpacked.

Why? Because so much of the holiday is traditional. The stockings, ornaments, and wreaths are all things that have been part of Christmas for hundreds of years, and some have roots going all the way back to ancient times. The Nordic countries of Denmark, Finland, Iceland, Norway, and Sweden have a rich folklore that also adds to today's traditions. They are all part of what makes Christmas, Christmas! People with a tradition of celebrating Christmas like seeing their own Christmas stockings again and again each year. They have ornaments and decorations that have been passed down in the family for generations. It is one of the few times when everyone can agree that old is definitely better than new.

Who started bringing trees inside?

History points to Germany as the place where the Christmas tree tradition began. The Germans didn't bring in the whole tree— just the top, which they would put on a table. It was then loaded with shiny ornaments, candy, and small presents. Over the years, presents got bigger and so did the tree, until a whole tree was put in a stand on the floor, leaving more room under the branches for gifts.

The practice of using lights on a tree may have come from ancient festivals when they used to place candles on fir trees—a beautiful but dangerous practice. The green of the fir branches and the light from the candles were symbols of the return of the sun and the growing season.

Today it is traditional to use electric lights to decorate our trees, both inside and outside. Large towns and cities often have trees they string with lights for the holiday.

Why do people decorate the outside of their houses?

There are some people who like to do everything in a big way. Decorating your house at Christmastime is one of those things. Up until about 1950, it wasn't practical to try to decorate the outside of the house. Lights were still expensive to buy, and if one bulb went out, the whole string of lights would go dark. Once that problem was solved, the idea of covering the house with lights caught on. Now some neighborhoods have house-decorating contests. The most elaborately decorated houses use as much as $4,000 worth of electricity to keep the lights on for the month of December.

Why do we hang stockings?

This is a tradition going straight back to St. Nicholas. There is a story that tells of a father with three daughters who could not marry. Back then, a bride needed to give her husband-to-be a dowry, which was something of value like money or jewelry. This father had nothing for his daughters to give. One night, St. Nicholas dropped a bag of gold through an open window. The next night another bag of gold was dropped in! The third night, the father stood at the window to catch who was leaving the gold.

Legend has it that St. Nicholas did not want to be seen, so he climbed to the roof and dropped the last bag of gold down the chimney, where it fell into a pair of stockings that were hung there to dry. The daughters had their dowries, and as this story was retold year after year, hanging stockings near the chimney became a Christmas tradition.

Christmas Stocking Magnet

Here is what you need:
- Old knit glove • Two tiny wiggle eyes
- Red, white, and green pipe cleaners
- Two small brown pom-poms
- One tiny red pom-pom • Cotton balls
- Small strip of gold or green rickrack
- Piece of sticky-back magnet
- Scissors • White tacky glue

Here is what you do:
1. Cut the longest finger from the glove to use as the stocking.
2. Fold a 6-inch (15-cm) piece of green pipe cleaner in half. Twist the ends together and shape a circle at the top.
3. Slip the twisted end of the pipe cleaner into the glove finger. Fold the pipe cleaner sideways at the base of the glove to form the foot of the stocking. Tip the circle at the top of the stocking to one side to form the hanger.
4. Lightly stuff the stocking with cotton to fill it.

5.   Cut a 2-inch (5-cm) piece of red and a 2-inch (5-cm) piece of white pipe cleaner. Twist the two pieces together to make a tiny candy cane. Fold the end over to form the hook of the candy cane. Rub some glue on the side of the bottom part of the candy cane and slip it down between the cotton and the inside of the stocking.

6.   To make a tiny teddy bear to peek out of the other side of the stocking, glue the pom-pom on the cotton next to the candy cane. Glue on small pom-pom ears, the two wiggle eyes, and a tiny pom-pom nose.

7.   Fluff out some cotton ball to glue around the top of the stocking for fur. Glue a strip of rickrack below the cotton.

8.   Press a piece of sticky-back magnet to the back of the stocking.

What's a Yule log?

There is more than one answer to this question. The first Yule log started as a Norse tradition. In the darkest days before the winter solstice, people would drag home the largest log they could manage. It had to be big enough to burn nonstop for twelve days, the length of the Norse winter feast known as Yule tide.

People still burn Yule logs in their fireplaces. In 1966, a New York television executive thought it would be nice for people without fireplaces to have a Yule log. He filmed a log fire, and it's still on TV for hours every Christmas Eve. Now you can put on a YouTube video to have a mini-Yule log on your computer in case you're afraid of the dark, like the Vikings!

Another answer to this question is that a Yule log is a special Christmas dessert. In France it is called a Bûche de Noël. It is a thin layer of cake rolled with cream filling and covered with icing. Some artistic bakers create bark and branches out of frosting.

Why do people send Christmas cards?

Today, Christmas cards with photographs are the most popular kind of card to send. People want to stay in touch with friends and family. Most families send and receive around twenty cards. This is nothing compared to the very first Christmas card ever sent. In 1843 Sir Henry Cole had 1,000 Christmas cards printed and hand-painted. Sir Cole did some projects for the British Postal Service so perhaps he had mail on his mind. The first mass-produced Christmas cards

looked more like Easter cards. They were covered with pastel colored flowers and fluttering birds.

Now, Christmas cards are very popular. Americans send almost 2 billion cards every Christmas!

Who thought of kissing under mistletoe?

This tradition started in England. People would hang balls of mistletoe as part of their holiday decorations. Any girl kissed under the mistletoe would supposedly be married in a year. But why mistletoe?

The answer lies in a story about Frigga, the Norse goddess of love. One day Frigga's son, Balder, told her he had dreamed that he was going to die. Frigga got a promise from everything that lived on earth that nothing would harm her son. But mistletoe does not grow on earth—it grows on trees and never touches the ground. A trickster god named Loki had an arrow made of mistletoe, and with it Balder was shot and killed. When Balder was returned to life the mistletoe was dedicated to Frigga. Her tears of joy became the mistletoe's white berries. Ever since, the plant—like others that stay green all year—has been a symbol of life and love.

Christmas Around the World

People around the world are different, liking different foods and speaking different languages. But a holiday like Christmas reminds us that the human family has more in common than we think. Today, Christmas is celebrated almost everywhere, although not always as an official holiday.

Most non-tropical countries have myths and legends that shaped the way they celebrate Christmas. The nativity story was also told and retold throughout history, and many countries created their own mythology around it.

Some countries, like Japan, have no winter mythology and no nativity story, as very few Japanese people are Christian. So they have created a celebration that is uniquely Japanese. Their Christmas cake is a sponge cake decorated with whipped cream and strawberries. Their trees are mostly artificial, with origami ornaments. They create fantastic light shows in public spaces, lighting not just trees but also making sculptures with lights. And for many Japanese people, their favorite Christmas dinner is Kentucky Fried Chicken. It's become a tradition for them. Their celebration may be different from yours, but it's all Christmas.

Who brings presents to children in other countries?

Santa Claus is a popular guy around the world and becomes more popular each year. But Santa Claus doesn't look the same in every country. And he has other names, such as St. Nicholas, Père Noël, La Befana, Baboushka, or Jultomten. They all look different from Santa, but they all are related to him. Many of them are characters in stories and folktales that explain who they are, how they look, and what they wear.

In Italy it's an old witch named La Befana. The Three Kings stopped at her house on the way to see the baby Jesus, but she was too busy sweeping to go with them. Now, once a year, she flies through the sky on her broom looking for the baby and bringing presents to children.

In Russia the winters are very cold and long. Father Frost brings gifts to children, helped by his granddaughter, the Snow Maiden. He is as strong as frozen water, and she is dressed all in white with a tiara of frozen crystals.

Swedish children look forward to the arrival of the jultomten. A tomte is a gnome with enormous strength and a bad temper, who helps with farm animals. A jultomten is a slightly less feisty tomte who

rides a straw goat to deliver presents. He still has a temper, and will be angry if he doesn't get a little porridge to eat when he visits a house.

Maybe the most unusual gift-giver is a camel. In Syria, the littlest camel from the Three Kings caravan delivers presents.

Does everyone leave cookies and milk for Santa on Christmas Eve?

Not exactly. Cookies and milk are an American tradition, but other countries welcome their gift-givers in different ways. Countries with colder climates, like Germany, Denmark, and Sweden, leave a bowl of porridge where St. Nicholas can find it.

In some countries people celebrate Epiphany, or Three Kings Day, on January 6. This is the day the three kings found baby Jesus. On the night before Epiphany, people have a tradition of leaving hay and carrots for St. Nicholas's horse, Santa's reindeer, or the animals that might have been present at the birth of Jesus. In these countries and others, many people believe that on the night Jesus was born all the animals present were given the gift of speech so they could welcome him. It's no wonder people are careful to leave food for such special creatures!

Who are Santa's helpers around the world?

In America, many people believe Santa has elves making toys at a workshop in the North Pole. Since they never leave the North Pole, no one has ever seen them. In some countries in Europe, the helpers are much more visible. In Austria, parts of Germany, and Croatia, St. Nicholas is accompanied by the Krampus, a super-scary, hairy wildman who punishes the naughty children while St. Nicholas gives the nice ones treats.

Garland Door Wreath

Here is what you need:
- 15-foot (4.5-meter) garland
- Heavy 9-inch (23-cm) paper plate
- Gold cord   • Red ribbon
- Scissors   • White tacky glue

Here is what you do:

1. Cut the center out of the paper plate. The rim will be the form for the wreath. If the plate feels flimsy glue two or three plate rims together to make a sturdy frame.
2. Secure one end of the garland to the plate with a dab of glue. Wrap the garland around and around the rim of the plate to cover it. Tuck the end of the garland under the wrapped garland and secure with a dab of glue.
3. Cut a 10-inch (25.5-cm) piece of gold cord for the hanger. Tie the cord around the wreath then tie the two ends together.
4. Use the red ribbon to make a bow. Glue the bow to the wreath to decorate.

Milk Cup and Cookie Plate for Santa

Here is what you need:

- Red, blue, or green plastic or paper disposable plate, bowl, and cup
- Paper fastener
- Ballpoint pen
- Sticker stars or Christmas stickers

Here is what you do:

1. Use the pen to poke a tiny hole in the center of the plate. Poke a second hole in the center of the bottom of the bowl.
2. Invert the bowl so that it becomes a pedestal for the plate. Use the paper fastener to attach the plate to the bowl through the two tiny holes.
3. Decorate the plate with sticker stars or Christmas stickers.
4. Decorate the cup to match.

What is an Advent calendar?

The word "advent" means "to come." Advent calendars are used to count down the days from December 1 until Christmas. They are often made of rectangular door cards with twenty-four little doors. Behind each is a picture of something relating to Christmas, with a special picture behind the final door meant to be opened on Christmas Eve.

The idea of using a special calendar for advent started in Germany, and the Germans still make the most beautiful advent calendars. People sometimes tape them to windows so as each door is opened the light shines through, illuminating the pictures that are revealed.

In the small town of Gengenbach, in Germany, there is a beautiful building with twenty-four windows. Every December the building is turned into a life-sized advent calendar. Each night until December 24 a new window is lit up. By Christmas Eve, the front of the building is ablaze in color and light.

What do kids around the world get for Christmas?

Presents, or at least the number and size of them, seem to be an American tradition for Christmas. Kids from lots of countries would be surprised to get a present on Christmas or on Epiphany, another holiday that celebrates Jesus' birth but is held on January 6.

Children in France, Great Britain, Canada, Finland, Poland, Japan, and the United States (all of whom do get presents) are very fond of writing Santa with their wish lists. Here is the address in case you want to write to Santa next year:

Santa Claus
Santa's Workshop Village
96930 Arctic Circle

FACT: Barbie is over fifty years old and still the most popular doll in the world. She is available in 150 different countries, and every three seconds, every day of the year, someone is getting a new Barbie doll.

Dark Beginnings

Imagine living back in a time when the only light at night came from the moon and stars, or from lighting a fire. On a dark night, looking beyond your fire's circle of light, you could believe the world had disappeared. Even scarier for our ancient ancestors was when the dark nights stayed dark longer, and the sun felt weaker each day. They didn't know why. They didn't know about the earth turning around the sun.

They didn't know that the sun would become stronger and the days would get longer again.

People began having ceremonies. They cursed whatever evil spirits might have made the sun go away. They begged their gods to bring the sun back. And it worked every time! The cold of winter always gave way to the warmth and light of spring.

About five thousand years ago people began to study the sky. After years of watching and thinking, they realized that on the shortest day of the year, the sun set far to the south. After that the days always began to grow brighter and warmer.

That shortest day of the year is now called the winter solstice. Once people knew exactly when the solstice was coming, their world was much less scary. Instead of cursing the long dark nights, people celebrated what they knew would be the return of the sun. These winter solstice celebrations were the earliest beginnings of what we now celebrate as Christmas.

Who decided when to celebrate Christmas?

When Christianity was a brand new religion, people were still celebrating the winter solstice. In ancient Rome and elsewhere, the celebration was called Saturnalia. It went on for days, sometimes weeks. People gave gifts. They decorated their homes and had lots of wild parties.

Then, in the year 312, Christianity was named the official religion of Rome. The Christian church officials knew they could not stop Saturnalia. People liked it too much. So they let the festival go on. But for Christians, this became a time to celebrate and honor the birthday of Jesus. And for everyone it remained, and still is, a celebration of friends, family, light, and the joy of life. It was not officially called Christmas until hundreds of years later.

Was Jesus really born on December 25?

No one really knows the exact date of Jesus's birth. December 25 was the birthday of the sun-god Mithras. He was the god of the official state religion of Rome before it was changed to Christianity. Mithras did not have a mother. He was born out of a rock. No women were allowed to be Mithrans. It was a popular religion with warriors, but plenty of people liked Christianity, too.

As part of changing Saturnalia to Christmas, the Emperor of Rome declared that instead of celebrating the birth of the sun-god Mithras on December 25, people would now celebrate the birth of the Son of God, Jesus Christ. Was it really the birthday of Jesus? Nope. Was anyone going to argue with the Emperor? Nope!

Shapes Nativity Scene

Here is what you need:

- 12-x-18-inch (30-x-46-cm) construction paper in all colors
- Printed paper scraps
- Facial tissue
- Black, brown, and yellow yarn
- Gold and silver trims
- Ribbon
- Collage items such as sequins, craft gems, and seed beads
- Cotton balls
- Pipe cleaners and sparkle stems
- Markers
- Sticker stars
- Scissors
- White tacky glue

Here is what you do:

1. Cut a triangle body and a circle head for each figure you wish to include in your nativity scene. To make a child figure use a shorter triangle. To make the baby Jesus use a tiny triangle and circle head. To make angel wings, add smaller triangles on each side of the figure.

2. Cut the point off a triangle and invert it for the manger. Cut two thin rectangles for legs and glue them across each other at the base of the manger.

3. Arrange the figures on a 12-x-18-inch (30-x-46-cm) sheet of paper. Secure them with glue.

4. Use printed paper and facial tissue to make headwear. If you need to slip it behind the heads you must do this before the glue dries.

5. Use markers to give each figure a face.

6. Use yarn bits to give each figure hair, and beards for the men. Use yellow yarn bits to make hay in the manger.

7. Use sparkle stems to make halos for the holy family and the angel. Glue them above the heads.

8. Use collage materials to decorate the figures.

9. Make a pipe cleaner crook and cotton ball lambs to glue in front of the shepherd. Glue a black paper face and ears on the front of each cotton ball lamb and glue seed bead eyes to the face.

10. Make crowns for the three kings from gold ribbon, gold trims, printed paper, and craft gems.

11. Tape together four 12-x-18-inch (30-x-46-cm) pieces of construction paper behind your scene with the edges sticking out evenly on the sides to create a frame for the scene.

12. Decorate the frame with collage materials such as ribbons and trims, gems, and sequins.

13. Cut a 2-foot (60-cm) piece of gold cord for a hanger. Glue one end to each side of the top of the back of the frame.

Have fun decorating the nativity scene in your own way!

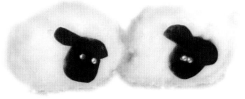

What's the nativity?

The nativity is the story of Jesus's birth. More than 2,000 years ago a baby was born in a small town in the hills of Palestine. Babies are born all the time. But according to the story in the Bible, there were signs to let people know this one was special. There were predictions from prophets, big, scary angels, a bright, unusual star in the sky, and a few months after the birth, the arrival of three kings bringing gifts—all for this one little baby in this small town in the hills.

Some towns and villages around the world put on living nativity plays today. They recreate the story with live animals and people who dress as

Joseph, Mary, baby Jesus, the three kings, the shepherds, and angels. People also put up creche* scenes in their houses. Whatever the real truth of Jesus's birth is, the nativity is a well-loved part of Christmas.

In a part of Spain called Catalonia, a favorite nativity figure is the caganer. This figure is pooping, and they always put him or her in the back of the scene so kids can have fun trying to find him.

FACT: The angels in Christianity that communicate with humans are archangels. They are grown-up sized, big, and strong. The first words they spoke to the shepherds in the nativity story were, "Be not afraid."

*Creche is a French word that means baby bed.

What were the first Christmas presents?

The three kings brought presents for the baby Jesus. Historians think that's what gave people the idea to give presents for Christmas. The presents we give now are nothing like the presents the kings brought. One king brought chunks of gold. Another brought frankincense, which is the dried sap of a particular kind of tree. It smells really good when it's burned to release the fragrance. The last king brought myrrh. That is dried tree sap, too. All three of these gifts were rare and valuable at the time.

When was the first Christmas in America?

The Puritans who came to America did not allow Christmas to be celebrated. They argued that the real birth date of Jesus wasn't even known, which is true. They said decorating with greens and bringing them into the house was pagan.* This is also true.

They were upset at the number of parties, and the over-the-top feasting and drinking that went on. They were right about that, too. Back then Christmas was not a quiet, family celebration. It was more like two weeks of vacation. The farming was done for the year and there was food in storage and less work to do in the quiet winter season.

Christmas eventually crept back onto the calendar, and it's probably here to stay.

*If you are Pagan, you believe in many gods, rather than just one like the Christians, Muslims, and Jews do.

Christmas Traditions, Superstitions, and Classics

Christmas Trivia

Ukrainian Christmas trees always have an ornament of a spider in a web for good luck.

In Greenland, a traditional Christmas food is kiviak. Here is the recipe: Take lots of auks, stuff them into a sealskin, and bury this in a box underground for several months. The auks will rot into a cheesy-something that supposedly tastes better than it smells.

In Oaxaca, Mexico, December 23 is the Night of the Radishes. Farmers grow radishes as big as two feet long, and artists carve them, making fantastic nativity scenes and other works of art. The red and white colors of the carved radishes make beautiful Christmas table decorations.

In Nuremberg, Germany, it is good luck to buy prune characters at the Christmas market, to bring luck into the house for the year.

Christmas in Canada would not be complete without Chicken Bones. They are a pink hard candy filled with chocolate or peanut butter, and are a Canadian Christmas tradition.

In Slovakia, a traditional Christmas food is loksa, which is bread pudding. Once the dough is made, they throw some up on the ceiling. The more loksa that sticks to the ceiling, the luckier the family will be.

Sweden's Christmas feast includes lutefisk, a dish in which fish is soaked in lye until it turns to a jelly-like texture. Not many people outside of Sweden develop a taste for it.

Classics to watch with your family

Home Alone (1990)

An eight-year-old boy is left behind when his family leaves for Christmas vacation. He has to protect his home against two robbers who do NOT know the meaning of Christmas.

It's a Wonderful Life (1946)

On Christmas Eve, an angel helps George Bailey realize that it is, indeed, a wonderful life.

A Christmas Story (1983)

All Ralphie wants for Christmas is a Red Ryder BB gun. Will it be under the tree on Christmas day?

The Polar Express (2004)

On Christmas Eve a boy who might not believe in Santa gets an amazing train ride to Santa's North Pole.

Classics to read with your family

A Christmas Carol
by Charles Dickens

How the Grinch Stole Christmas!
by Dr. Seuss

The Gift of the Magi
by O. Henry

Nutcracker
by E. T. A. Hoffman, with pictures
by Maurice Sendak

Is there anyone who doesn't love Christmas?

Christmas can be a hard time for some people. If you don't have money to buy presents, it can make you sad. Some people are upset that Christmas is not more religious. But nobody hates Christmas like Scrooge. Fortunately, he is just a character in a book.

In 1843 an author named Charles Dickens wrote a book called *A Christmas Carol*. He imagined a character, Ebenezer Scrooge, who did not know the meaning of Christmas. He was such a mean old man it didn't seem possible that he could change. Thanks to some ghostly visits, Scrooge did change, and by the end of the book, he learned that giving to others can be like a gift to yourself.

Two other famous Christmas bad guys are the Grinch and the White Witch of Narnia. The Grinch tries to steal Christmas and the White Witch made it winter all year long without a Christmas. You can read about them in the books *How the Grinch Stole Christmas!* by Dr. Seuss, and *The Lion, the Witch and the Wardrobe*, by C. S. Lewis.

Christmas Cookie Recipe

One thing many people look forward to at Christmas time is Christmas cookies! It is as much fun to make and decorate them as it is to eat them. A classic Christmas cookie is Gingerbread Men. If you don't have gingerbread-men-shaped cookie cutters, you can use cutters shaped like stars, Christmas trees, or even just a round glass. The last make excellent ornament-shaped cookies. If you poke a hole near the edge before baking, you can hang the cookie on the tree!

Ingredients:

3 cups flour
¼ teaspoon salt
¾ teaspoon baking soda
2 teaspoons ground ginger
1 teaspoon ground cinnamon
¼ teaspoon ground nutmeg
¼ teaspoon ground cloves
½ cup unsalted butter, room temperature
½ cup sugar

1 egg
⅔ cup molasses

Here is what you do:
1. Mix flour, salt, baking soda, and the spices together in a bowl.
2. In a large bowl, use an electric mixer to mix the butter and sugar until light and fluffy. Add the egg and molasses, and mix again. Then slowly add the flour mixture while beating (this takes a helper.)
3. Refrigerate the dough for two hours.
4. Preheat the oven to 350°F. Cover two baking sheets with parchment paper or silpats.
5. Cut the dough and put half on flour sprinkled on the counter to keep it from sticking. With a flour-sprinkled roller, roll the dough until it's about ¼-inch thick. Use a cookie cutter to cut out your cookies.
6. Bake 8–10 minutes in the oven (ask an adult to put the cookies in the hot oven).
7. Use store-bought frosting and small candy to decorate.

Merry Christmas to Everyone!

In Italy say, "Buon Natale"
    (Bwon– na-TA-lee)

In Mexico and Spain say, "Feliz Navidad"
    (fe-LEESE NAH-VEE–dad)

In Hawaii say, "Mele Kalikimaka"
    (Mel–ee Ka-lick-ee-MAKA)

In England say, "Happy Christmas"

In Japan say, "Merii Kurisumasu"
    (Merry Kur-EE-su-ma-su)

In South Africa say,
    "Geseënde Kersfees"
    (Es-ee-enn-da KASH-fe-us)

In France say, "Joyeux Noël"
    (Zhway-uh No-el)

In Sweden say, "God Jul"
    (Good Yule)

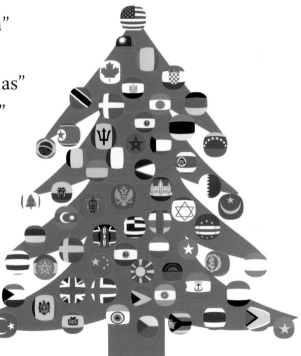

What can people do to give everyone a Merry Christmas?

In *A Christmas Carol*, Scrooge is reminded that giving is better than receiving. There are lots of groups that do a good job giving to others, and they all need help, especially at Christmas time. If you're feeling a little Scroogy, try these ideas:

1. Check at your school to see if any clubs are having a holiday fundraiser that you can help with. Get the word out—maybe other clubs will join in.

2. Ask your librarian to help you find local charities you might want to help at during the season.

3. Check with local supermarkets. Sometimes they have food drives. You could make posters to remind people to buy extra canned goods to drop in the food drive boxes.

4. Local churches and shelters often have Christmas dinners for people who don't have enough to eat. Volunteer to help collect food or serve the meal.

5. Tell your mom and dad you want to trade one or two of your presents for a donation to a cause of your choice.

6. Drop your pocket change in the red kettles of the Salvation Army. They have been doing good works since 1891.

7. Toys for Tots is run by the United States Marine Corps Reserves. They donate toys to children. You can find out where to donate a toy by going to the Toys for Tots website: www.toysfortots.org/.

8. Another charity, Heifer International, helps people around the world help themselves. You can chip in to buy a goat or chickens that will help a family start a new life: www.heifer.org.

9. Oxfam Unwrapped has a long list of unusual gifts that help people in need: www.oxfamamericaunwrapped.com.

Bibliography

Chalmers, Irena. *The Great American Christmas Almanac: A Complete Compendium of Facts, Fancies, and Traditions*. New York: Viking Studio Books, 1988.

Del Re, Gerard, and Patricia. *The Christmas Almanack*. New York: Doubleday and Company, 1979.

Eliade, Mircea. *The Encyclopedia of Religion, Volume 3: Christianity*. New York: Macmillan, 1987.

Elliot, Jock. *Inventing Christmas: How Our Holiday Came To Be*. New York: Harry N. Abrams, 2002.

Forbes, Bruce David. *Christmas: A Candid History*. California: University of California Press, 2007.

Green, Jonathan. *Christmas Miscellany: Everything You Always Wanted to Know About Christmas*. New York: Skyhorse Publishing, 2009.

Hadfield, Miles, and John. *The Twelve Days of Christmas*. Boston: Little Brown and Company, 1961.

Hutchison, Ruth, and Ruth Adams. *Every Day's a Holiday*. New York: Harper & Row, 1951.

Lankford, Mary D. *Christmas Around the World*. New York: William Morrow and Company, 1995.

Nissenbau, Stephen. *The Battle for Christmas*. New York: Alfred A. Knopf, 1996.

Pfeffer, Wendy. *The Shortest Day: Celebrating the Winter Solstice*. New York: Dutton Books, 2003.

Stevens, Patricia Bunning. *Merry Christmas: A History of the Holiday*. New York: Macmillan, 1979.

Index